one
sentence
a day

one
sentence
a day

a mindful journal

quadrille

my name is:

_____

my age is:

_____

one quality I like about myself is:

_____

_____

_____

_____

one quality I would like to improve
about myself is:

_____

_____

_____

_____

in case of loss, theft or any other
accident, please return to:

_____

_____

_____

draw a self-portrait here:

how to use
this book

This journal is designed for you to reflect each day on the most meaningful thing that happens to you. This exercise, drawing inspiration from the practice of mindfulness, allows you to step back from the distractions of modern life, and focus on what's truly important to you. By writing one sentence a day for a whole year, you will discover, perhaps unexpectedly, the moments, people and experiences that have impacted your mood and mindset the most.

Some of your sentences may be mundane – small snapshots of an unremarkable day – while others are momentous. This journal is an opportunity to celebrate both. On re-reading your journal, you will be confronted with a wealth of memories, large and small, which together will help build the mosaic of your year: a panoramic picture of the things you value most.

To make the most of this mindful journal, start by choosing a consistent time each day for reflection. It could be a quiet moment in the morning, a brief pause during lunch, or a serene evening routine. Find a comfortable space where you can be alone with your thoughts, free from the noise of the outside world.

As you sit down to write, let the process be a form of self-care. Allow yourself the luxury of introspection and the simplicity of recording a single sentence. There's no need for elaborate prose or perfection; instead, focus on authenticity. Your entries are fragments of your journey, capturing the essence of each unique day.

A number of additional prompts appear throughout the book, encouraging you to reflect on your recent experiences and how they have impacted you. Don't feel you have to fill in these pages in order – if the words don't come naturally in the moment, come back to them when inspiration strikes. Some days, your sentences may flow effortlessly, encapsulating moments of joy or newly-found insights. Other days, they may be less profound. Embrace the diversity of your sentences, for within them lies the richness of your existence.

As you progress through the days and weeks, notice the evolving narrative of your life. Your sentences will weave together to create a narrative that reflects your growth, resilience, and gratitude. This mindful journal is a companion on your journey, a mirror that reflects the layers of your identity, and a treasure trove of memories that will become more precious with time. Embrace the simplicity, celebrate the complexity, and let each sentence be a step towards a more mindful and intentional life.

inital reflections

the person that means the most to me is

_____

_____

the place that i feel happiest is

_____

_____

my favourite book is

_____

_____

my favourite song is

_____

_____

my favourite film is

_____

_____

my last 3 courses on earth would be

_____

_____

_____

one thing i am proud of is

_____

_____

_____

one thing i want to achieve
in the next 12 months is

_____

_____

_____

daily
reflections

the most *meaningful* part of my day

_____

day

day

day

day

the most
meaningful
part of my day

day

day

day

day

the most *meaningful* part of my day

day
_____
_____
_____
_____
_____

day

day

day

the most *meaningful* part of my day

day

_____

_____

_____

_____

day

day

day

the most *meaningful* part of my day

day
_____
_____
_____
_____
_____

day

_____
_____
_____
_____
_____

day

_____
_____
_____
_____
_____

day

_____
_____
_____
_____
_____

10 things that bring me *joy*

1 _____

2 _____

3 _____

4 _____

5 _____

6 _____

7 _____

8 _____

9 _____

10 _____

day

day

day

day

the most
meaningful
part of my day

the most *meaningful* part of my day

day

_____

_____

_____

_____

_____

day

day

day

the most *meaningful* part of my day

day

day

day

day

the most *meaningful* part of my day

day

day

day

day

the most *meaningful* part of my day

day

_____
_____
_____
_____
_____

day

_____

_____

_____

_____

_____

day

_____

_____

_____

_____

_____

day

_____

_____

_____

_____

_____

1

2

3

4

5

5 things
I've *enjoyed*
doing recently

the most *meaningful* part of my day

day

_____

_____

_____

_____

_____

day

day

day

the most *meaningful* part of my day

day

_____

_____

_____

_____

_____

day

day

day

the most *meaningful* part of my day

day

_____

_____

_____

_____

day

_____

_____

_____

_____

day

_____

_____

_____

_____

day

_____

_____

_____

_____

the most *meaningful* part of my day

day

_____
_____
_____
_____
_____

day

day

day

the most *meaningful* part of my day

day

day

day

day

the last
trip I took

the most *meaningful* part of my day

day

_____

_____

_____

_____

_____

day

day

day

the most *meaningful* part of my day

day

_____

_____

_____

_____

day

day

day

day

day

day

day

the most
meaningful
part of my day

_____

the most *meaningful* part of my day

day
_____
_____
_____
_____
_____

day

day

day

the most *meaningful* part of my day

day

_____

_____

_____

_____

day

_____

_____

_____

_____

day

_____

_____

_____

_____

day

_____

_____

_____

_____

my top 5
sentences
from the
last 10 pages

1

2

3

4

5

the most *meaningful* part of my day

day

day

day

day

the most *meaningful* part of my day

day

_____

_____

_____

_____

_____

day

day

day

the most *meaningful*
part of my day

day

_____

_____

_____

_____

day

_____

_____

_____

_____

day

_____

_____

_____

_____

day

_____

_____

_____

_____

the most *meaningful* part of my day

day

day

day

day

the most *meaningful* part of my day

day

_____
_____
_____
_____
_____

day

day

day

what I am
most looking
forward to

today

_____
_____
_____
_____
_____

this week

_____
_____
_____
_____
_____

this month

_____
_____
_____
_____
_____

this year

_____
_____
_____
_____
_____

day

day

day

day

the most
meaningful
part of my day

———————————————————

the most *meaningful* part of my day

day

_____

_____

_____

_____

_____

day

day

day

the most *meaningful* part of my day

_____

day

day

day

day

the most
meaningful
part of my day

day

day

day

day

the most *meaningful* part of my day

day

_____

_____

_____

_____

_____

day

day

day

the last thing
I heard, read
or saw that
inspired me

heard

_____

_____

_____

_____

read

_____

_____

_____

_____

saw

_____

_____

_____

_____

the most *meaningful* part of my day

day
_____
_____
_____
_____
_____

day

day

day

the most *meaningful* part of my day

day

_____

_____

_____

_____

_____

day

day

day

the most *meaningful* part of my day

day

day

day

day

the most *meaningful* part of my day

day
_____
_____
_____
_____
_____

day

day

day

day

day

day

day

the most
meaningful
part of my day

_____

one
thing...

I am proud of

_____

_____

_____

_____

_____

how I achieved it

_____

_____

_____

_____

_____

what it means to me

_____

_____

_____

_____

_____

the most *meaningful* part of my day

day

_____

_____

_____

_____

_____

day

day

day

day

_____

_____

_____

_____

day

_____

_____

_____

_____

day

_____

_____

_____

_____

day

_____

_____

_____

_____

the most
meaningful
part of my day

the most *meaningful* part of my day

day

_____

_____

_____

_____

day

day

day

the most
meaningful
part of my day

day

_____

_____

_____

_____

day

_____

_____

_____

_____

day

_____

_____

_____

_____

day

_____

_____

_____

_____

the most *meaningful* part of my day

day

---

day

day

day

my most
memorable
dream

_____

the most *meaningful* part of my day

day
_____
_____
_____
_____
_____

day

_____

_____

_____

_____

_____

day

_____

_____

_____

_____

_____

day

_____

_____

_____

_____

_____

the most *meaningful* part of my day

day
_____
_____
_____
_____
_____

day

day

day

day

day

day

day

the most
meaningful
part of my day

the most *meaningful* part of my day

day

_____

_____

_____

_____

_____

day

day

day

the most
meaningful
part of my day

day

---

day

---

day

---

day

---

a conversation
I have found
interesting
recently

———————————————

the most *meaningful* part of my day

day

_____
_____
_____
_____
_____

day

day

day

the most
meaningful
part of my day

day

_____

_____

_____

_____

day

_____

_____

_____

_____

day

_____

_____

_____

_____

day

_____

_____

_____

_____

the most *meaningful* part of my day

day

_____

_____

_____

_____

_____

day

---

day

---

day

---

the most
meaningful
part of my day

day

day

day

the most *meaningful* part of my day

day

_____

_____

_____

_____

_____

day

day

day

day

my top 5
sentences
from the
last 10 pages

1

2

3

4

5

the most
meaningful
part of my day

day

_____

_____

_____

_____

_____

day

_____

_____

_____

_____

_____

day

_____

_____

_____

_____

_____

day

_____

_____

_____

_____

_____

the most *meaningful* part of my day

day

_____

_____

_____

_____

_____

day

day

day

the most *meaningful* part of my day

day
_____
_____
_____
_____

day

_____

_____

_____

_____

_____

day

_____

_____

_____

_____

_____

day

_____

_____

_____

_____

_____

the most
meaningful
part of my day

day

_____

_____

_____

_____

_____

day

_____

_____

_____

_____

_____

day

_____

_____

_____

_____

_____

day

_____

_____

_____

_____

_____

the most *meaningful* part of my day

day

_____
_____
_____
_____
_____

day

day

day

day

my favourite
day from the
last 10 days

the most *meaningful* part of my day

day

_____
_____
_____
_____
_____

day

_____

_____

_____

_____

_____

day

_____

_____

_____

_____

_____

day

_____

_____

_____

_____

_____

the most *meaningful* part of my day

day

_____

_____

_____

_____

_____

day

_____

_____

_____

_____

_____

day

_____

_____

_____

_____

_____

day

_____

_____

_____

_____

_____

day

_____

_____

_____

_____

day

_____

_____

_____

_____

day

_____

_____

_____

_____

day

_____

_____

_____

_____

the most
meaningful
part of my day

the most *meaningful* part of my day

day

day

day

day

the most *meaningful* part of my day

day

_____

_____

_____

_____

_____

day

day

day

day

the last time I...

laughed

---

cried

---

felt ecstatic

---

was angry

---

day

_____

_____

_____

_____

day

_____

_____

_____

_____

day

_____

_____

_____

_____

day

_____

_____

_____

_____

the most
meaningful
part of my day

---

the most *meaningful* part of my day

day

_____

_____

_____

_____

_____

day

_____

_____

_____

_____

day

_____

_____

_____

_____

day

_____

_____

_____

_____

day

_____

_____

_____

_____

the most *meaningful* part of my day

day

_____

_____

_____

_____

_____

day

_____

_____

_____

_____

_____

day

_____

_____

_____

_____

_____

day

_____

_____

_____

_____

_____

the most *meaningful* part of my day

day

day

day

day

the most *meaningful* part of my day

day
_____
_____
_____
_____
_____

day

_____

_____

_____

_____

_____

day

_____

_____

_____

_____

_____

day

_____

_____

_____

_____

_____

I want to...

_____

see more of

go to

do more of

the most
meaningful
part of my day

day

_____

_____

_____

_____

_____

day

_____

_____

_____

_____

_____

day

_____

_____

_____

_____

_____

day

_____

_____

_____

_____

_____

the most *meaningful* part of my day

day

_____
_____
_____
_____
_____

day

day

day

day

day

day

day

day

the most
meaningful
part of my day

_____

the most
meaningful
part of my day

day

day

day

day

the most *meaningful* part of my day

day

_____

_____

_____

_____

_____

day

_____

_____

_____

_____

_____

day

_____

_____

_____

_____

_____

day

_____

_____

_____

_____

_____

10 things I want to do but haven't yet

1 _____

2 _____

3 _____

4 _____

5

6

7

8

9

10

the most *meaningful* part of my day

day

_____

_____

_____

_____

_____

day

_____

_____

_____

_____

day

_____

_____

_____

_____

day

_____

_____

_____

_____

the most *meaningful* part of my day

day

_____
_____
_____
_____
_____

day

day

day

day

the most
meaningful
part of my day

day

_____
_____
_____
_____

day

_____
_____
_____
_____

day

_____
_____
_____
_____

day

_____
_____
_____
_____

day

day

day

day

the most
meaningful
part of my day

————————————————

the most *meaningful* part of my day

day

_____

_____

_____

_____

_____

day

_____

_____

_____

_____

_____

day

_____

_____

_____

_____

_____

day

_____

_____

_____

_____

_____

what's on my reading list...

draw your bookshelf

the most
meaningful
part of my day

day

_____

_____

_____

_____

day

_____

_____

_____

_____

day

_____

_____

_____

_____

day

_____

_____

_____

_____

the most *meaningful* part of my day

day

_____

_____

_____

_____

_____

day

day

day

day

the most *meaningful* part of my day

day

day

day

day

the most *meaningful* part of my day

day

_____

_____

_____

_____

_____

day

_____
_____
_____
_____
_____

day

_____
_____
_____
_____
_____

day

_____
_____
_____
_____
_____

day

_____
_____
_____
_____

day

_____
_____
_____
_____

day

_____
_____
_____
_____

day

_____
_____
_____
_____

the most *meaningful* part of my day

top 5 places
I have visited
this year

1

2

3

4

5

the most *meaningful* part of my day

day

_____

_____

_____

_____

day

_____

_____

_____

_____

day

_____

_____

_____

_____

day

_____

_____

_____

_____

the most *meaningful* part of my day

day
_____
_____
_____
_____

day

_____

_____

_____

_____

_____

day

_____

_____

_____

_____

_____

day

_____

_____

_____

_____

_____

the most *meaningful* part of my day

day

_____

_____

_____

_____

_____

day

day

day

day

day

day

day

day

the most
meaningful
part of my day

_____

the most
meaningful
part of my day

_____

day

day

day

day

10 things
I want to
achieve

1 _____
_____
_____

2 _____
_____
_____

3 _____
_____
_____

4 _____
_____
_____

5

6

7

8

9

10

the most *meaningful* part of my day

day

_____

_____

_____

_____

_____

day

day

day

day

the most
meaningful
part of my day

day

day

day

day

the most
meaningful
part of my day

day

_____

_____

_____

_____

_____

day

_____

_____

_____

_____

_____

day

_____

_____

_____

_____

_____

day

_____

_____

_____

_____

_____

the most *meaningful* part of my day

day

_____

_____

_____

_____

_____

day

day

day

day

day

day

day

the most
meaningful
part of my day

_____

the most
meaningful
part of my day

day

day

day

day

the most
meaningful
part of my day

day

_____

_____

_____

_____

_____

day

day

day

day

my *favourite* sentence in my journal

final reflections

the person that means the most to me is

_____

_____

the place that i feel happiest is

_____

_____

my favourite book is

_____

_____

my favourite song is

_____

_____

my favourite film is

_____

_____

my last 3 courses on earth would be

_____

_____

_____

one thing i am proud of is

_____

_____

_____

one thing i want to achieve
in the next 12 months is

_____

_____

_____

look over your answers on the previous page and compare them to your initial reflections at the start of this journal.

have any of your answers changed?

_____

☐ yes   ☐ no

why do you think that is?

space to stick in
meaningful memories

space to stick in
meaningful memories